ANIMAL LIVES

LIONS

Sally Morgan

QED

QED Publishing

Designed and edited by Calcium

First published in the UK in 2014 by QED Publishing
A Quarto Group company
The Old Brewery, 6 Blundell Street
London, N7 9BH

www.qed-publishing.co.uk

A catalogue record for this book is available from the British Library.

ISBN: 978 1 78171 522 2

Printed in China

Photo credits
(t=top, b=bottom, l=left, r=right, c=centre, fc=front cover)

Alamy 6–7 Top-Pics TBK 15t Afripics; **Corbis** fc Anup Shah; **FLPA** 4–5 Ariadne Van Zandbergen, 8–9 Winfried
Wisniewski/Minden Pictures, 9t Konrad Wothe/Imagebroker, 10–11 Ingo Arndt/Minden Pictures, 11t Suzi
Eszterhas/Minden Pictures, 11b Frans Lanting, 12–13 Malcolm Schuyl, 13t Michel and Christ/Biosphoto, 13b
Malcolm Schuyl, 14-15 Shem Compion, 16-17 Bernd Rohrschneider, 16b Michel and Christ/Biosphoto, 18-19
Frans Lanting, 19b Elliott Neep, 20-21 Mitsuaki Iwago/Minden Pictures, 21b Michel and Christi/Biosphoto, 22-23
Christian Heinrich/Imagebroker, 23b Imagebroker, 24-25 Elliott Neep, 25t Imagebroker, 26-27 Vincent Grafhorst/
Minden Pictures, 27t Imagebroker, 27b Elliott Neep, 28-29 Frans Lanting, 29t Suzi Eszterhas/Minden Pictures, 29b
Andrew Parkinson, 32 Mitsuaki Iwago/Minden Pictures; **Getty Images** 2–3 Grant Faint; **Shutterstock** 1 Maggy
Meyer, 5t Dennis Donohue, 7b Mogens Trolle, 17t Johan du Preez, 30t MDD, 30l Jason Prince, 30br Maggy Meyer,
31 Eric Isselee, bc(l) Vishnevskiy Vasily, bc(r) Eric Isselee.

Contents

The lion

The lion is a big cat and is related to tigers, cheetahs and leopards. All these cats are skilful hunters that eat meat. Lions belong to a group of animals called mammals. Mammals are animals that have hair and produce milk for their young.

A family of lions is called a pride.

Male manes

It is easy to identify a male lion (right) because he has a thick mane around his head. The mane makes males look big and also protects their necks during fights.

A female lion is known as a lioness, and her young are called cubs.

FANTASTIC FACT

Male lions weigh about 200 kilograms. Lionesses weigh about 150 kilograms.

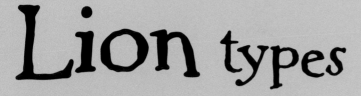

Lion types

There is only one species, or type, of lion. However, there are slight variations between lions living in different parts of the world, so the lion species is divided into five groups called **subspecies**. They are the Angolan, Asiatic, Masai, Senegalese and Transvaal lions.

Types of lion

Subspecies	Where they live
Angolan	Zimbabwe, Angola and the Congo
Asiatic	Gir Forest in India
Masai	East Africa
Senegalese	West Africa
Transvaal	South Africa

FANTASTIC FACT

Lions are the second largest living cat species, second only to the tiger.

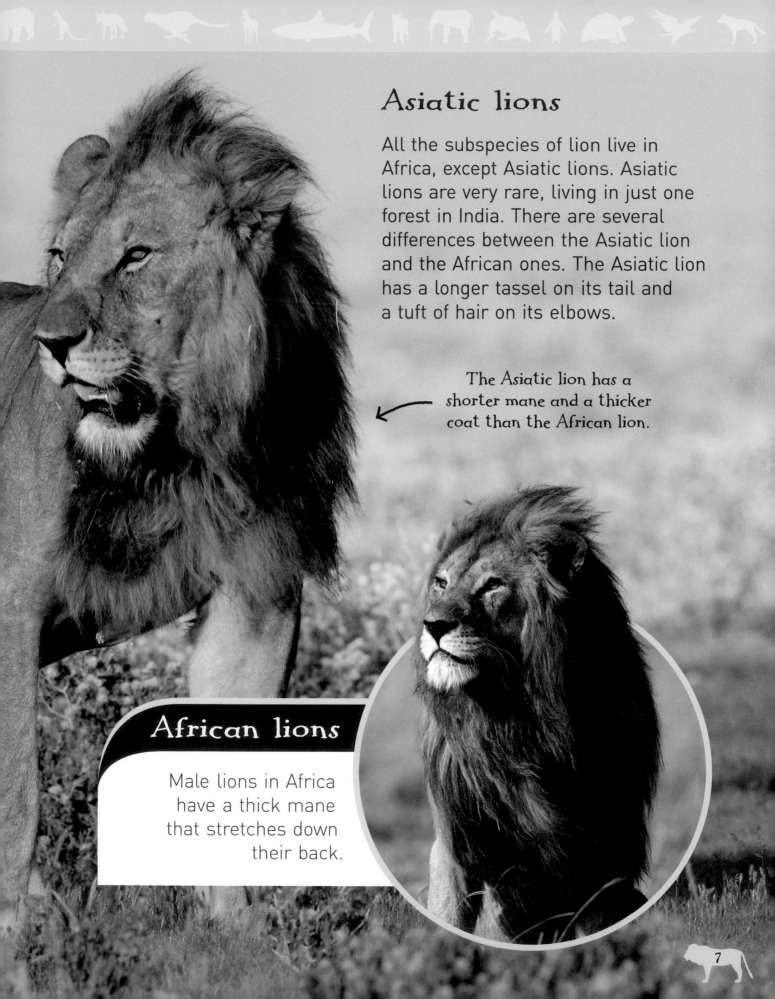

Asiatic lions

All the subspecies of lion live in Africa, except Asiatic lions. Asiatic lions are very rare, living in just one forest in India. There are several differences between the Asiatic lion and the African ones. The Asiatic lion has a longer tassel on its tail and a tuft of hair on its elbows.

The Asiatic lion has a shorter mane and a thicker coat than the African lion.

African lions

Male lions in Africa have a thick mane that stretches down their back.

Where lions live

In the past, lions were found in more places than they are today. They roamed across Africa, southern Europe, the Middle East and as far east as India. Now they are found only in parts of Africa and India. All African lions live south of the Sahara Desert. The Asiatic lion can only be found in the Gir Forest in northwestern India.

Lion habitats

Most African lions live on the **savannah** – a flat grassland with few trees. The lions share the savannah with grazing animals, such as antelope, zebras and wildebeests. Lions kill and eat these animals.

Europe

Asia

Africa

Atlantic Ocean

Indian Ocean

Around the world

The areas in pink on this map show where lions live.

Lions in India

In India, lions live in a forest **habitat** rather than on the savannah. They eat deer that live in the forest.

There are few places to hide on the savannah. A lion's yellow coat makes it hard to spot in the long, dry grass.

FANTASTIC FACT

Two thousand years ago, gladiators in Rome often fought lions in public arenas. Christians were also fed to lions in the arenas.

Living in a pride

Lions live in groups called **prides**. A typical pride is made up of between 4 and 12 lionesses, their cubs and up to 6 adult males. The lionesses are all related, but none of them are related to the pride's adult males.

Territories

The pride lives in an area called a **territory**. However, the lions in a pride do not stay together all of the time. They form smaller groups and wander throughout the territory. They come together only occasionally.

A pride of lions work together to look after the young and to find food.

FANTASTIC FACT

When a male lion or group of males takes over a pride, they kill all the youngest cubs. The male leader mates with the lionesses to produce their own young.

Fighting over territory

Adult male lions defend their
territory from other males
who would like to take it over.

Lazing about

Lions spend much of their
day asleep in the shade.

Beginning life

After mating, the lioness is **pregnant** for about 15 weeks. The cubs are very small, weighing only 2 kilograms, when they are born. There are normally two or three cubs in a litter, and the lioness feeds the cubs with her milk.

Meeting the pride

When a cub is two months old, it is introduced to the other lions in the pride. The younger cubs are left together in a nursery group. The adult lionesses take it in turns to look after them.

FANTASTIC FACTS

Newborn cubs weigh just one-hundredth of the weight of an adult lion.

. . . .

Only one in every four lion cubs survives to become an adult.

Hungry cubs rush up to a lioness to drink her milk.

Keeping safe

The lioness has to hide her cubs in a safe place when she goes hunting. She carries them gently by the neck to a hiding place.

Keeping hidden

Every few days a lioness mother moves her cubs to a new hiding place, in case **predators** have spotted them.

Growing up

Lion cubs feed on their mother's milk for about six months. They grow teeth when they are three months old and begin to eat meat. When the pride kills an animal, the cubs are taken to it by their mother to practise chewing on meat.

Play–fighting

Playing helps cubs to learn hunting and fighting skills. When they are one year old, the cubs are allowed to follow the lionesses on a hunt. At first the youngsters only watch, but soon they begin to take part.

During play-fights, lion cubs do not really bite or scratch each other. They just pretend.

Stay or go?

When they become adults, lionesses stay with the pride, but the male lions (right) are driven away once they are about three years old. Often they join other males of the same age and form a male-only group.

FANTASTIC FACT

A lioness will give milk to her sisters' and cousins' cubs as well as her own.

Predators

The lionesses do most of the hunting. They are strong enough to kill **prey** that is as large as they are. Their claws are long, strong and curved, to hook into a victim's flesh. Males sometimes also hunt and kill prey, such as wildebeests.

Super strong jaws

Lions have strong jaws to lock around the neck of their prey and kill it.

Different teeth

Lions have four types of teeth. The small incisors at the front are for nibbling meat off bones. At the corners of the mouth are four curved canine teeth, which are used to stab prey. Behind the canines are large premolars and molars that slice through meat and bone like scissors.

FANTASTIC FACT

The lion's tongue is so rough, it has a texture like sandpaper. It is used to scrape bits of meat off bones.

Lions cannot run fast over long distances. They have to sneak up close to their prey before dashing in for the kill.

Lion senses

Lions usually hunt at dusk and dawn, when the sun is low. The lion's prey can't see as well in the dim light, but a lion's senses of sight, smell and hearing are perfect for hunting.

The lion's large eyes glow in the dark, just like a pet cat's.

FANTASTIC FACT

Lion cubs have blue eyes, but they change to amber when they are older.

Excellent eyesight

A lion's eyes are the biggest of any cat. They point forward – this helps them to judge distances well. This is especially useful when a lion is chasing and leaping onto prey. A lion's eyes are very sensitive to movement. This means that if an animal stays really still, the lion will probably not spot it.

Hearing

Lions turn their head in the direction of a sound in order to hear it better. Their ears can twist slightly, too, and this helps them to find out exactly where the sound is coming from.

Lion movement

Lions are large animals but they can charge forward at speeds of 50 kilometres per hour for a short distance. A lioness can run faster than a male lion. Her body is better suited to hunting, whereas the male's heavier body is better suited to fighting.

Lions run with a series of long bounds.

FANTASTIC FACT

Lions can leap 9 metres – that is almost as long as a bus.

Silent walking

Lions can walk almost silently. Under each of their toes is a pad that cushions the paws and softens any noise. Their claws can be pulled back, or **retracted**, inside their toes when they are not being used. This protects the claws from being worn down.

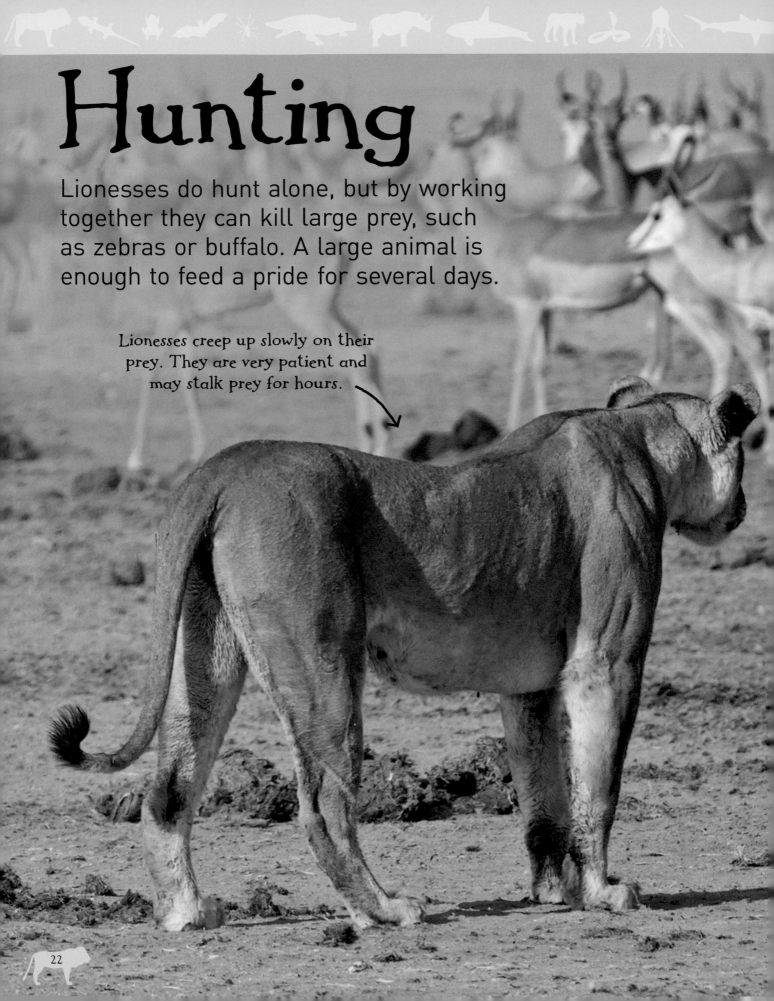

Hunting

Lionesses do hunt alone, but by working together they can kill large prey, such as zebras or buffalo. A large animal is enough to feed a pride for several days.

Lionesses creep up slowly on their prey. They are very patient and may stalk prey for hours.

Different roles

At the start of a hunt, the lionesses spread out in a fan. Some lionesses walk towards the prey, forcing it in the direction of the other lionesses that are hidden in the grass. These lionesses ambush the prey when it is close enough. The lionesses kill it by biting its neck to stop it breathing.

Males first

The male lions are always the first to feed. Once they have finished, the females feed, and then finally the cubs are allowed to eat.

Living in a territory

A pride of lions lives in an area called a territory. The size of the territory depends on how much food is available. If there is plenty of prey, the territory is small. In less crowded places, the lions can occupy much larger areas. Large territories can be as big as 400 square kilometres.

Smell defence

Male lions patrol the territory. They mark trees and boulders with their **urine**. The smell of the urine tells other lions to keep away.

If lions from different prides meet, they will often fight and inflict serious injuries on each other.

FANTASTIC FACT

Lions often share their territory with other predators, such as cheetahs and leopards.

Communication

At dawn and dusk, the roar of lions can be heard across the savannah. Roaring is one way that lions keep in contact with each other. Male lions roar to warn other males to keep away. Lionesses use roars to call their cubs. To communicate with each other, lions also moan, grunt, snarl and growl.

FANTASTIC FACTS

A lion's roar can be heard up to 8 kilometres away.

. . . .

Both lions and lionesses communicate by roaring.

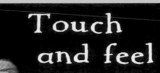

Touch and feel

Body contact is very important to lions. Lions of the same pride greet each other by rubbing their cheeks together. Sometimes they rub their necks and bodies against each other, too.

Grooming

During quiet times of the day, pride members often lick each other. This is called grooming. It cleans the fur, removes ticks and fleas and also helps lions in a pride to stay friends.

Lions under threat

In the past, people went on safari in Africa to shoot wildlife, not to look at it. Even today, some people still pay to shoot lions just for fun. For this reason, and many others, the number of lions in the wild is falling.

In danger

Other threats to lions include farming and diseases. As the number of people in Africa increases, more of the savannah is used for farming. Dogs belonging to local people also spread diseases to the lions.

FANTASTIC FACTS

Ten years ago there were 100,000 lions in Africa, but now there are just 17,000.
. . . .
Just 200 Asiatic lions are left in the protected Gir Forest.

The territories where lions live are increasingly under threat.

Conservation

Areas of African savannah are now under **conservation**. They have been made into national parks, where the wildlife is protected. Tourists visiting the parks bring money into the area, which can be used to help local people and to protect lions.

Tracking lions

This lioness is wearing a transmitter. This will allow scientists to trace her movements.

Life cycle of a lion

A lioness is ready to breed by the time she reaches three years old. She gives birth to a litter of two or three cubs. The lionesses stay with the pride, but the young males are chased away. A lion may live for 15 years in the wild, but as many as 25 years in a zoo.

cub

older cub

adult

Glossary

conservation protecting wildlife from being damaged by the activities of humans

habitat the place where an animal or plant lives

predators animals that hunt and eat other animals

pregnant a female animal that has a baby or babies developing inside her

prey an animal that is hunted by other animals

prides groups of lions that live together

retracted pulled in, as a cat can pull in its claws

savannah a grassy plain found in tropical parts of the world

scavenge to feed on the dead and decaying bodies of animals

subspecies groups within a species that look slightly different from each other

territory an area where a lion spends its life and where it finds all of its food

urine water that is passed out of the body of a mammal

Index